I LOVE RUNNING

Notebook (7 x 10 Inches)

A Penelope Pewter Production

This Notebook Belongs To:

Phone:

E-Mail:

www.InspirationalWares.com

HABIT/GOAL TRACKER

Start Date:

Habit/Goal	1	2	3	4	5	6	7	8	9	10	11	12	13	14	15	16	17	18	19	20	21	22	23	24	25

For more amazing journals and adult coloring books from Penelope Pewter, visit:

Amazon.com
CreateSpace.com
RWSquaredMedia.Wordpress.com

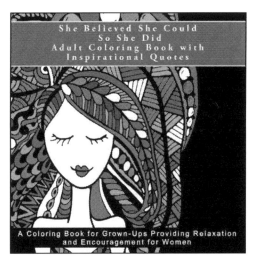

She Believed She Could
So She Did Adult Coloring Book
with Inspirational Quotes

The Be A Pineapple Adult
Coloring Book

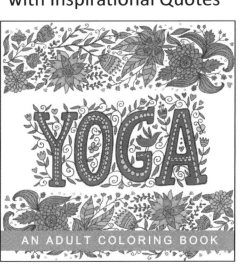

YOGA
An Adult Coloring Book

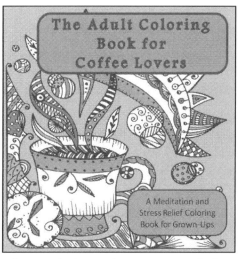

The Adult Coloring Book for
Coffee Lovers

InspirationalWares.com

Funny & inspirational calendars, posters, coffee mugs and more!

https://InspirationalWares.com

Printed in Great Britain
by Amazon